THE CHARLIE KIRK'S STORY

Charting The Rise and Challenges of a Conservative Icon, From The Beginning of His Career to an Amazing Family Life

By

Susan Cloff

Table of Contents

Introduction..6

Chapter 1...16

  Roots of a Rebel - The Early Years...........................16

    Growing Up in Arlington Heights and Prospect Heights, Illinois...17

    Early Political Engagement - Supporting Mark Kirk's Senate Campaign..21

    The Spark of Activism - Campaigning Against School Cafeteria Price Hikes..24

    Meeting Bill Montgomery and the Influence of the Tea Party Movement...26

    Decision to Forgo Traditional College for Political Activism 29

Chapter 2...34

  Founding a Movement - The Rise of Turning Point USA.........34

    Co-founding Turning Point USA with Bill Montgomery in 2012...35

    Building a National Student Movement for Free Markets and Limited Government 39

    Strategies for Engaging Young Conservatives - Campus Activism and Media Presence 43

    Early Triumphs and Challenges in Establishing TPUSA's Influence..47

    Recognition as a Young Conservative Leader - Forbes "30 under 30" and RNC Appearances 51

Chapter 3 56

Navigating the Political Storm - Leadership and Controversies 56

Confrontations with Progressive Critics and Navigating
Political Polarization 57

Key Controversies - Views on the Civil Rights Act, COVID-
19, and Climate Change 61

Involvement in the January 6 Events and the House Select
Committee Investigation 66

Balancing Leadership of Turning Point Action, Academy, and
Faith Initiatives...69

The Evolution of Kirk's Public Stance and Media
Controversies...73

Chapter 4 78

Media Maverick - Building a Conservative Voice 78

The Charlie Kirk Show - From Podcast to Top-Ranked Apple
News Podcast 79

Establishing a Media Empire - Radio, Social Media, and
Salem News Channel...82

Crafting a No-Holds-Barred Conservative Narrative for a
Digital Audience..86

Impact of Social Media Reach - Over 100 Million Monthly
Engagements 89

Authoring Books - From Campus Battlefield to Right Wing
Revolution 92

Chapter 5 98

Beyond the Spotlight - Family Life and Legacy.......................98

Personal Milestones - Marriage, Family, and Balancing Public
and Private Life 99

The Man Behind the Movement - Kirk's Personal Evolution
and Values 102

Building a Lasting Conservative Legacy Through Grassroots
Activism 105

Inspiring the Next Generation - The Role of Family and Faith
in Kirk's Vision 109

Reflections on the Future of Conservatism and Kirk's
Ongoing Influence..112

Conclusion 116

Introduction

The journey of human progress has always been shaped by the interplay of ideas, actions, and the environments in which they unfold. This book explores the forces that drive transformation in individuals, communities, and societies, examining how innovation, resilience, and collaboration converge to create meaningful change. It is a reflection on the patterns of human endeavor—how people adapt, create, and overcome challenges to build a future that reflects their highest aspirations. Through stories, insights, and analysis, the following pages uncover the dynamics that propel humanity forward, offering a lens to understand the past, navigate the present, and shape what lies ahead.

At the heart of this exploration is the recognition that progress is not a straight line. History shows that advancements often emerge from struggle, uncertainty, and the willingness to question established norms. From the agricultural revolutions that reshaped ancient societies to the technological breakthroughs of the modern era, human ingenuity has consistently found ways to transcend limitations. For example, the development of the steam engine in the 18th century did not merely power machines; it redefined economies, connected distant regions, and altered the way people lived and worked. Similarly, the rise of the internet in the late 20th century transformed communication, commerce, and access to knowledge, creating opportunities that were unimaginable just decades earlier. These milestones illustrate a recurring theme: innovation often stems from a blend of necessity, curiosity, and the courage to experiment.

Yet, progress is not solely the domain of inventors or pioneers. It is equally driven by ordinary individuals who, through small but deliberate actions, contribute to the larger mosaic of change. Consider the grassroots movements that have reshaped societal norms, such as the civil rights campaigns of the 1960s or the global push for environmental sustainability in recent decades. These efforts demonstrate that collective action, rooted in shared values, can challenge entrenched systems and inspire lasting impact. This book examines these dynamics, highlighting how individual choices and collective efforts intersect to create moments of transformation.

The structure of the book is designed to offer a comprehensive yet accessible exploration of these themes. It begins by tracing the historical roots of innovation, drawing on examples from diverse cultures and eras to illustrate how ideas take hold and spread. From the ancient trade routes that connected civilizations to the modern digital networks that link billions, the exchange of knowledge has always been a catalyst for growth. The narrative then shifts to the present, analyzing how contemporary challenges—such as climate change, economic inequality, and technological disruption—are shaping the decisions individuals and societies make today. Finally, it looks to the future, exploring the possibilities and uncertainties that await, from advancements in artificial intelligence to the potential for global cooperation in addressing shared problems.

One of the central arguments is that change is not inevitable; it is shaped by choices. Societies that thrive are those that foster environments where creativity, collaboration, and adaptability are valued. For instance, the rapid development of vaccines during the COVID-19 pandemic showcased what is possible when scientists, governments, and communities work together under pressure. In less than a year, researchers developed multiple effective vaccines, a feat that would have been unthinkable without decades of prior research, global coordination, and public trust. This example underscores the importance of preparation, cooperation, and the ability to act decisively in the face of uncertainty.

The book also considers the role of resilience in navigating challenges. Human history is replete with examples of societies that faced existential threats—whether natural disasters, economic collapse, or conflict—and emerged stronger through adaptation. The rebuilding of Japan after World War II, for instance, transformed a devastated nation into a global economic powerhouse within decades. This resilience was not merely a product of resources but of a collective commitment to renewal, education, and innovation. By examining such cases, the book highlights the qualities that enable individuals and communities to not only survive but thrive in the face of adversity.

Another key focus is the interplay between technology and human values. As tools like artificial intelligence, biotechnology, and renewable energy reshape the world, they raise profound questions about ethics, equity, and responsibility. The development of autonomous vehicles, for example, promises to reduce accidents and improve mobility, but it also prompts debates about privacy, job displacement, and decision-making in life-or-death scenarios. These tensions are not new; every major technological shift, from the printing press to the telegraph, has sparked similar questions. By exploring these issues, the book seeks to provide a framework for understanding how societies can balance progress with the principles that define their humanity.

The narrative is grounded in real-world examples, drawing on stories from diverse contexts to illustrate universal themes. From the entrepreneurs in sub-Saharan Africa using mobile technology to expand access to education, to the indigenous communities in the Americas preserving traditional knowledge while embracing sustainable practices, these stories highlight the breadth of human experience. They also underscore a critical point: progress is not a one-size-fits-all phenomenon. What constitutes advancement in one context may not apply in another, and understanding these nuances is essential to fostering inclusive growth.

The book also addresses the role of leadership in driving change. Effective leaders, whether in politics, business, or community organizing, share a common trait: the ability to inspire others to act toward a shared goal. Historical figures like Nelson Mandela, who bridged divides to unite a fractured nation, or modern leaders like those spearheading renewable energy initiatives, demonstrate how vision and empathy can galvanize action. Yet leadership is not confined to those in positions of power. Everyday individuals—teachers, activists, parents—often play equally pivotal roles in shaping their communities. By highlighting these stories, the book celebrates the power of agency at every level of society.

Education emerges as another recurring theme. Knowledge is the foundation of progress, enabling individuals to understand their world and imagine new possibilities. The expansion of literacy in 19th-century Europe, for instance, fueled social and economic mobility, while today's digital learning platforms are democratizing access to education across the globe. However, disparities in access to education persist, particularly in underserved regions. The book examines how addressing these gaps can unlock human potential and drive collective advancement.

Throughout, the narrative emphasizes the importance of collaboration. No major challenge—whether eradicating disease, mitigating climate change, or fostering economic opportunity—can be addressed in isolation. The Paris Agreement of 2015, for example, represented a global commitment to tackling climate change, even if its implementation has faced hurdles. Such efforts highlight the necessity of aligning diverse interests toward a common purpose. The book explores how partnerships, whether between nations, organizations, or individuals, can amplify impact and create solutions that endure.

The exploration is not without its sobering moments. Progress often comes at a cost, and the book does not shy away from examining the trade-offs. Industrialization lifted millions out of poverty but also contributed to environmental degradation. Digital connectivity has empowered communities but also amplified misinformation and division. By grappling with these complexities, the book encourages you to approach progress with both optimism and critical awareness, recognizing that every advancement carries responsibilities.

Ultimately, this book is an invitation to reflect on the forces that shape the world and the role each person plays in that process. It is a call to engage with the challenges and opportunities of the present while keeping an eye on the horizon. The stories, ideas, and insights offered here aim to inspire a deeper understanding of what it means to build a better future—not just for some, but for all. By examining the past, analyzing the present, and imagining what lies ahead, the book seeks to equip you with the perspective needed to navigate an ever-changing world.

The pages that follow offer a journey through time, ideas, and human experience. They explore how innovation sparks change, how resilience overcomes obstacles, and how collaboration turns possibilities into realities. Above all, they affirm a simple yet profound truth: the future is not something that happens to humanity—it is something humanity creates. Through understanding, action, and shared purpose, that creation can reflect the best of what people are capable of achieving together.

Chapter 1

Roots of a Rebel - The Early Years

The journey to becoming a force in political activism often begins in the unlikeliest of places—small towns, suburban neighborhoods, or moments of youthful defiance that ignite a lifelong passion. In the quiet suburbs of Chicago, where tree-lined streets and community traditions shaped daily life, a young mind found inspiration not in grand events but in the everyday challenges and opportunities of a close-knit community.

This chapter traces the formative years of an individual whose path to influence began in the ordinary yet vibrant settings of Arlington Heights and Prospect Heights, Illinois. It explores how early experiences in these towns, combined with a growing awareness of political and social issues, set the stage for a bold decision to step away from conventional paths and embrace a life of activism. From local campaigns to personal encounters that reshaped ambitions, these early years reveal the seeds of a rebel spirit, ready to challenge norms and pursue a vision of change.

Growing Up in Arlington Heights and Prospect Heights, Illinois

The suburbs of Arlington Heights and Prospect Heights, nestled just northwest of Chicago, offered a quintessential American upbringing in the 1990s and early 2000s. Arlington Heights, with its bustling downtown and historic charm, was a place where families gathered for community events like the annual Frontier Days festival, complete with parades, carnival rides, and local bands. Prospect Heights, smaller and more residential, provided a quieter backdrop, with sprawling parks and tight-knit neighborhoods. Together, these towns created an environment that balanced suburban tranquility with access to the cultural and economic pulse of Chicago. For a young person growing up here, life was shaped by the rhythms of school, family, and community involvement, but also by a growing awareness of the broader world.

Arlington Heights, with a population of around 75,000 during the 1990s, was a hub of middle-class stability. Its schools, part of District 214, were known for their academic rigor and extracurricular opportunities. Wheeling High School, where the subject of this narrative studied, was a microcosm of the area's diversity, drawing students from both Arlington Heights and Prospect Heights. The school's sprawling campus, with its mix of modern facilities and aging classrooms, reflected the community's pride in education but also its occasional struggles with funding and resources. Growing up in this environment meant navigating a world where community values were strong, but tensions over taxes, school budgets, and local governance were never far from the surface.

Prospect Heights, with fewer than 17,000 residents, offered a more intimate setting. Its neighborhoods, dotted with ranch-style homes and cul-de-sacs, fostered a sense of belonging. Local parks like John Muir Park were gathering spots for families, where kids played soccer or rode bikes while parents discussed local issues. The town's proximity to O'Hare International Airport meant the occasional roar of planes overhead, a reminder of its connection to the wider world. For a teenager, these towns provided both security and a subtle push toward curiosity about life beyond their borders. The subject's family, with a father working as an architect and a mother focused on mental health counseling, embodied the professional yet community-oriented ethos of the area.

Scouting played a significant role in shaping character during these years. As a member of the Boy Scouts of America, the subject earned the rank of Eagle Scout, a process that required years of dedication, leadership, and community service. Organizing projects like park cleanups or food drives instilled a sense of responsibility and a knack for mobilizing others—skills that would later prove invaluable in activism. The scouting experience, rooted in the values of duty and preparedness, also exposed the young individual to debates about tradition, patriotism, and civic engagement, which were particularly resonant in the conservative-leaning suburbs of the time.

The cultural and political climate of Arlington Heights and Prospect Heights during the 2000s was shaped by their proximity to Chicago, a Democratic stronghold, yet tempered by the more conservative leanings of suburban voters. Local newspapers like the **Daily Herald** frequently covered debates over property taxes, school funding, and infrastructure, reflecting the concerns of residents who valued fiscal responsibility and local control. For a teenager coming of age in this environment, these issues were not abstract but part of the fabric of daily life—heard in conversations at the dinner table, at community meetings, or in the pages of the local paper. This setting laid the groundwork for a keen interest in how decisions were made and who held power, setting the stage for early political engagement.

Early Political Engagement - Supporting Mark Kirk's Senate Campaign

By 2010, during the junior year of high school, the subject's interest in politics took a concrete form through involvement in the U.S. Senate campaign of Illinois Republican Mark Kirk (no relation). The campaign, which aimed to secure the seat once held by Barack Obama, was a high-stakes contest in a state known for its political volatility. Mark Kirk, a moderate Republican with a background in the U.S. House of Representatives, positioned himself as a pragmatic conservative, appealing to suburban voters wary of both Democratic overreach and the rising influence of the Tea Party. For a 16-year-old in

Arlington Heights, volunteering for this campaign was an entry point into the world of political organizing.

The campaign's local efforts were centered in places like Arlington Heights, where volunteers canvassed neighborhoods, distributed yard signs, and organized phone banks. The subject's involvement included door-to-door canvassing, a task that required confidence and a quick grasp of the candidate's platform, which emphasized fiscal responsibility, national security, and job creation. These experiences offered a firsthand look at grassroots politics—meeting voters, hearing their concerns, and learning to articulate a candidate's message. The campaign's success, with Mark Kirk narrowly defeating Democrat Alexi Giannoulias in November 2010, was a formative moment, proving that dedicated effort could influence outcomes in a competitive race.

The political climate of 2010 was charged with energy from the Tea Party movement, which had gained traction nationwide. In Illinois, the movement's influence was evident in the enthusiasm of conservative voters, who were frustrated with government spending and the Affordable Care Act. While Mark Kirk was not a Tea Party candidate, his campaign benefited from this wave of conservative activism, which resonated with many in the suburbs. For the subject, exposure to these ideas through campaign events and discussions with volunteers sparked an interest in the broader conservative movement, even as the campaign itself focused on mainstream Republican priorities.

This early engagement was not without challenges. Balancing schoolwork with campaign activities required discipline, and navigating the diverse opinions of voters—some supportive, others skeptical or hostile—taught resilience. The experience also highlighted the power of local action in shaping national outcomes, as Illinois's Senate race drew attention from across the country. The subject's role, though modest, instilled a sense of agency and a belief that individual efforts could contribute to larger causes, a lesson that would shape future endeavors.

The Spark of Activism - Campaigning Against School Cafeteria Price Hikes

In the senior year at Wheeling High School, a seemingly mundane issue—the rising cost of cafeteria cookies— became the catalyst for a first foray into activism. The school administration, facing budget pressures, had increased prices for cafeteria items, a move that frustrated students already navigating the social and academic challenges of high school. For the subject, this was not just a minor inconvenience but an opportunity to challenge authority and rally peers around a shared cause.

The campaign against the price hike was grassroots in every sense. It began with conversations in the cafeteria, where students voiced their irritation at paying more for snacks they had come to expect as affordable. The subject took the lead in organizing a response, gathering signatures for a petition and speaking at school board meetings to argue that the price increase unfairly burdened students, many of whom relied on cafeteria food as a primary source of nutrition. The effort was not about cookies alone but about fairness, transparency, and the principle that students deserved a voice in decisions affecting their daily lives.

This campaign required creativity and persistence. Posters appeared around the school, urging students to join the cause, and informal meetings in the library or after class helped coordinate efforts. The subject's ability to mobilize classmates, many of whom were initially apathetic, demonstrated an early knack for leadership. The campaign culminated in a partial victory: while the price of cookies was not fully reversed, the school board agreed to review its budget and consider student input in future decisions. This outcome, though modest, was a powerful lesson in the impact of collective action and the importance of challenging decisions that seemed arbitrary or unfair.

The experience also exposed the subject to the inner workings of local governance. School board meetings, often attended by a handful of parents and teachers, became a classroom in civic engagement. Listening to debates about budgets, union contracts, and property taxes revealed the complexities of public administration and the competing interests at play. For a teenager, these insights were a revelation, showing how local issues connected to broader political and economic debates. The campaign against cafeteria price hikes, though small in scope, planted the seeds of a broader commitment to questioning authority and advocating for change.

Meeting Bill Montgomery and the Influence of the Tea Party Movement

A pivotal moment came in 2012, during a speaking engagement at Benedictine University's "Youth Empowerment Day" in Lisle, Illinois. There, the subject met Bill Montgomery, a retiree and Tea Party-backed legislative candidate whose passion for conservative principles left a lasting impression. Montgomery, in his

50s and a seasoned activist, saw potential in the young high school senior and offered mentorship that would redirect the course of a life.

Montgomery was a figure emblematic of the Tea Party movement, which had surged in influence since 2009. Frustrated with government overreach, high taxes, and deficit spending, the Tea Party resonated with many in Illinois's suburbs, where residents often felt squeezed by state and local taxes. Montgomery's message centered on limited government, individual liberty, and fiscal responsibility—ideas that aligned with the subject's growing skepticism of centralized authority. Their conversations, which began at the event and continued in the weeks that followed, were a crash course in conservative ideology, from the writings of Milton Friedman to the principles of the Founding Fathers.

The Tea Party's influence was particularly strong in Illinois in 2012, as activists organized rallies and supported candidates challenging the state's Democratic dominance. Montgomery introduced the subject to local Tea Party gatherings, where discussions about the national debt, healthcare reform, and Second Amendment rights were common. These meetings were not just ideological echo chambers but vibrant forums where ordinary citizens—small business owners, retirees, and parents—debated policy and strategy. For an 18-year-old, the energy of these gatherings was electrifying, offering a sense of belonging to a movement that felt both urgent and righteous.

Montgomery's encouragement to pursue activism full-time was a turning point. He argued that the subject's passion and organizational skills—honed through scouting, the cafeteria campaign, and the Senate race—could have a greater impact outside the traditional paths of college and career. This advice resonated at a time when the subject was already questioning the value of a conventional education in a rapidly changing world. Montgomery's mentorship provided not just ideological grounding but also practical guidance, from how to speak to an audience to how to build a network of supporters. This relationship laid the foundation for a bold decision to prioritize activism over the expected trajectory of college and a stable career.

Decision to Forgo Traditional College for Political Activism

After graduating from Wheeling High School in 2012, the subject faced a choice that would define the future: pursue a traditional college education or dive into the uncertain world of political activism. The decision to forgo college was not made lightly but was driven by a combination of personal conviction, external influences, and a belief that the moment demanded action over preparation. This choice, unconventional for a high-achieving student with an Eagle Scout background, reflected a growing disillusionment with the traditional path and a desire to make an immediate impact.

The subject briefly enrolled at Harper College, a community college in Palatine, Illinois, in the fall of 2012. Harper was a practical choice, offering affordable courses and proximity to home. However, the classroom environment felt disconnected from the urgency of the political moment. The Tea Party's rise, the 2012 presidential election, and debates over healthcare and economic policy dominated the national conversation, and the subject felt compelled to engage directly rather than study from the sidelines. Part-time online courses at The King's College in New York City were also attempted, but the pull of activism proved stronger.

Montgomery's influence was critical in this decision. He argued that the skills needed for activism—public speaking, organizing, and strategic thinking—were better learned through experience than in a lecture hall. The subject's exposure to conservative thinkers, through Montgomery's recommendations and events like the 2012 Republican National Convention, further reinforced this view. At the convention, interactions with activists and donors, including prominent Republican supporter Foster Friess, highlighted the potential for a young voice to make a difference in a movement hungry for new energy.

The decision was also shaped by a broader cultural shift. In the early 2010s, stories of young entrepreneurs and activists bypassing college to pursue unconventional paths were gaining attention. Figures like Peter Thiel, who offered fellowships to encourage young people to skip college and start businesses, challenged the notion that a degree was the only path to success. For the subject, the opportunity to found an organization—Turning Point USA, launched in 2012 with Montgomery's support—offered a chance to channel passion and skills into a tangible mission: mobilizing young conservatives to counter liberal influence on campuses and beyond.

Forgoing college was not without risks. Friends and family expressed concern about financial stability and the lack of a degree as a fallback. Yet the subject's experiences—

organizing for Mark Kirk, leading the cafeteria campaign, and connecting with Montgomery—had built confidence in the ability to navigate uncertainty. The founding of Turning Point USA, with its focus on grassroots organizing and conservative values, marked the culmination of these early years. It was a bold leap, driven by a belief that the time for action was now, not after years of study.

The early years in Arlington Heights and Prospect Heights were more than a backdrop; they were a crucible for a rebel spirit. From the community pride of scouting to the political awakening of a Senate campaign, from the small victory of a cafeteria protest to the transformative mentorship of Bill Montgomery, these experiences shaped a young person's path. The decision to forgo college was not a rejection of learning but a commitment to a different kind of education—one rooted in action, conviction, and a vision for change. These roots, planted in the suburbs of Chicago, would grow into a movement that sought to reshape the political landscape, driven by the lessons of youth and the courage to chart an unconventional course.

Chapter 2

Founding a Movement - The Rise of Turning Point USA

The early 2010s marked a turning point in American political culture, as a wave of grassroots energy reshaped the conservative landscape. In the suburbs of Chicago, a young activist, barely out of high school, seized this moment to launch an organization that would galvanize a generation. This chapter traces the origins and rapid ascent of Turning Point USA, a movement born from a vision to empower young people with the ideas of free markets and limited government.

From its humble beginnings in a basement office to its emergence as a national force, the story of Turning Point USA is one of ambition, strategy, and resilience. It explores how a partnership between a seasoned mentor and a determined teenager sparked a movement, the innovative approaches that captured the attention of young conservatives, and the triumphs and obstacles that defined its early years. Through media savvy, campus organizing, and high-profile recognition, the organization's leader carved out a place as a prominent voice in the conservative movement, setting the stage for a broader impact.

Co-founding Turning Point USA with Bill Montgomery in 2012

In June 2012, just days after graduating from Wheeling High School in Illinois, an 18-year-old activist partnered with Bill Montgomery, a retired marketing entrepreneur and Tea Party supporter, to launch Turning Point USA. The organization was founded with a clear mission: to promote conservative values among young people, particularly on high school and college campuses. This partnership, born from a chance meeting at Benedictine University's "Youth Government Day" in Lisle, Illinois, combined Montgomery's experience and resources with the youthful energy and vision of his protégé. The result was a nonprofit that aimed to challenge the perceived liberal dominance in education and inspire students to embrace principles of free markets and limited government.

Montgomery, then in his early 70s, brought a wealth of business acumen to the endeavor. Born in Lincoln, Nebraska, in 1940, he had built a career in marketing, publishing, and restaurant management before retiring to focus on conservative activism. His involvement in the Tea Party movement, which gained momentum in 2009, gave him a network of like-minded activists and a deep commitment to reducing government overreach. At the Benedictine event, Montgomery was struck by the young speaker's ability to articulate conservative ideas with clarity and conviction. Describing the speech as "practically Reaganesque," he saw an opportunity to mentor a new voice in the conservative movement. Their conversations quickly turned to action, and Montgomery urged the young activist to forgo college and dedicate himself to political organizing full-time.

The founding of Turning Point USA was a modest affair, launched from a small office in Lemont, Illinois, with Montgomery handling the legal and financial paperwork as the organization's secretary and treasurer. The 501(c)(3) nonprofit status allowed the group to operate as a tax-exempt entity, focusing on education and advocacy rather than direct political campaigning. Montgomery's role was critical in the early days, as he navigated the complexities of nonprofit regulations, secured initial funding, and provided strategic guidance. Meanwhile, the young co-founder became the public face of the organization, speaking at local events and building a network of supporters. Their complementary skills— Montgomery's behind-the-scenes expertise and the activist's charisma—set the foundation for a movement that would soon expand beyond Illinois.

The timing of the launch was significant. In 2012, the United States was in the midst of a contentious presidential election, with President Barack Obama facing Republican challenger Mitt Romney. The Tea Party's influence was at its peak, fueling debates about government spending, healthcare reform, and individual liberty. This political climate provided fertile ground for an organization targeting young people, many of whom felt disconnected from traditional political institutions. Turning Point USA positioned itself as a fresh, youth-driven alternative, aiming to rival liberal groups like MoveOn.org by mobilizing students around conservative ideals. The partnership between Montgomery and his young co-founder was not without its challenges—generational differences and strategic disagreements occasionally surfaced—but their shared commitment to the cause kept the organization focused. By the end of 2012, Turning Point USA had begun to establish a presence on a handful of local campuses, laying the groundwork for a national movement.

Building a National Student Movement for Free Markets and Limited Government

Turning Point USA's mission to promote free markets and limited government resonated with a generation of students navigating a post-recession economy and growing skepticism about centralized authority. The organization sought to create a national network of student activists who could advocate for conservative principles on campuses, which were often seen as strongholds of progressive ideology. This ambitious goal required a strategic approach to organizing, messaging, and outreach, with a focus on empowering young people to take ownership of their political beliefs.

The early strategy centered on establishing chapters at colleges and high schools across the country. Unlike traditional conservative organizations, which often relied on top-down leadership, Turning Point USA adopted a grassroots model, encouraging students to form their own chapters and tailor activities to their campuses. By 2013, the organization had a presence on over 100 campuses, a number that would grow to 1,000 by 2015. These chapters organized events, distributed literature, and hosted speakers to promote ideas like deregulation, free enterprise, and individual responsibility. The slogan "Big Government Sucks" became a rallying cry, blending irreverence with a clear rejection of bureaucratic overreach. This approach appealed to students who saw themselves as outsiders challenging the academic establishment.

Funding was a critical component of the organization's growth. Early support came from conservative donors who saw potential in the youth-focused model. At the 2012 Republican National Convention in Tampa, Florida, the young co-founder met Foster Friess, a Wyoming businessman and prominent Republican donor. Impressed by the vision for a student movement, Friess provided initial financial backing, which allowed Turning Point USA to hire staff and expand its reach. Other donors, including the Ed Uihlein Family Foundation and the

Lynde and Harry Bradley Foundation, followed, providing resources to support campus events and national conferences. By 2016, the organization's revenue had reached $4.3 million, a testament to its ability to attract wealthy supporters.

The movement's growth was also fueled by its focus on economic issues that resonated with young people. The 2008 financial crisis had left many students wary of government intervention, while rising college tuition and student debt highlighted the limitations of centralized solutions. Turning Point USA's messaging emphasized free markets as a path to prosperity, drawing on thinkers like Milton Friedman and Ronald Reagan to argue that reducing government involvement would unleash innovation and opportunity. Events like the Student Action Summit, launched in 2013, brought together hundreds of students for workshops, speeches, and networking, reinforcing the organization's commitment to empowering young conservatives. By 2015, these summits were attracting thousands, with attendees from every state.

The organization also tapped into the cultural frustrations of young conservatives, who often felt marginalized on liberal-leaning campuses. Chapters organized provocative events, such as "affirmative action bake sales" to critique race-based policies or "tax day" protests to highlight government waste. These activities were designed to spark debate and draw attention to conservative ideas, often generating media coverage that amplified the movement's reach. By framing its mission as a defense of free speech and individual liberty, Turning Point USA positioned itself as a counterforce to what it saw as academic indoctrination, resonating with students who felt their views were stifled.

Strategies for Engaging Young Conservatives - Campus Activism and Media Presence

Engaging young conservatives required a blend of innovative tactics and a keen understanding of the digital age. Turning Point USA's strategies focused on two key pillars: campus activism and a robust media presence. These approaches not only mobilized students but also elevated the organization's profile, making it a leading voice in the conservative youth movement.

Campus activism was the heart of Turning Point USA's strategy. The organization trained student leaders to organize events, recruit members, and engage their peers in discussions about conservative principles. The National Field Program, established in 2013, provided resources like branded literature, posters, and talking points to help chapters make an impact. Students were encouraged to set up tables in high-traffic areas, such as campus quads, to distribute materials and start conversations. These tabling efforts often used bold slogans like "Socialism Sucks" or "Gen Z is Gen Free" to catch attention and provoke reactions. By 2015, the program employed 17 full-time staff to support chapters, a number that grew to over 350 by 2021.

Events were another cornerstone of campus activism. Chapters hosted speakers, debates, and protests to challenge progressive narratives and energize conservative students. For example, in 2014, the "Big Government Sucks" campaign went viral on social media, with students sharing photos of themselves holding signs at campus events. These efforts were designed to be both educational and confrontational, encouraging students to question prevailing campus ideologies. The organization also created the Professor Watchlist in 2016, a controversial initiative that documented professors accused of promoting "leftist propaganda" or discriminating against conservative students. While criticized for targeting academics, the list drew significant attention and reinforced Turning Point USA's image as a defender of free speech.

Media presence was equally important in reaching young conservatives. The organization's leader became a frequent guest on conservative outlets like Fox News, CNBC, and Breitbart, where he articulated the case for free markets and limited government. A 2012 appearance on **Fox and Friends** to discuss the youth vote marked an early milestone, followed by a segment on Neil Cavuto's show during the Republican National Convention. These appearances not only raised the organization's profile but also established its leader as a charismatic spokesperson for young conservatives. By 2015, he had appeared on national television over 100 times, a remarkable feat for a 21-year-old.

Social media was a game-changer for Turning Point USA's outreach. The organization embraced platforms like Twitter, Facebook, and Instagram to share memes, videos, and infographics that distilled conservative ideas into shareable content. A 2014 campaign criticizing President Obama's economic policies used memes to reach millions, blending humor with political messaging. This approach resonated with a generation raised on digital media, helping the organization build a following among students who might not attend rallies but engaged online. By 2016, Turning Point USA's social media accounts had tens of thousands of followers, amplifying its message far beyond campus borders.

The organization also invested in high-profile events to attract media attention. The Young Women's Leadership Summit, launched in 2018, and the Young Black Leadership Summit, started in 2019, targeted specific demographics while showcasing the diversity of the conservative movement. These events featured prominent figures like Donald Trump Jr. and Lara Trump, drawing thousands of attendees and generating extensive coverage in conservative media. By combining campus activism with a sophisticated media strategy, Turning Point USA created a feedback loop that energized students and amplified its influence.

Early Triumphs and Challenges in Establishing TPUSA's Influence

The rise of Turning Point USA was marked by significant triumphs that solidified its place in the conservative movement, but it also faced challenges that tested its resilience. The organization's ability to navigate these highs and lows shaped its early trajectory and demonstrated its adaptability.

One of the earliest triumphs was the rapid expansion of campus chapters. By 2015, Turning Point USA had established a presence on over 1,000 campuses, a remarkable achievement for an organization founded just three years earlier. This growth was driven by the energy of student leaders, who organized events that drew hundreds of attendees. The 2014 "Big Government Sucks" campaign was a standout success, with students across the country hosting protests and sharing content that reached millions online. The campaign's irreverent tone and focus on economic freedom resonated with young people, earning praise from conservative leaders like Foster Friess and Peter Huizenga, who donated $50,000 to the organization in 2014.

Another triumph was the organization's ability to attract high-profile supporters. At the 2016 Republican National Convention in Cleveland, the young leader's speech as the youngest speaker in attendance drew national attention. The event also marked a pivotal connection with Donald Trump Jr., who became a frequent speaker at Turning Point USA events. This relationship elevated the organization's profile and aligned it with the rising MAGA movement, helping it secure funding from donors like the Koch-affiliated Foundation for Economic Education and DonorsTrust. By 2016, the organization's revenue had grown to $4.3 million, enabling it to hire additional staff and expand its programs.

However, the rapid growth brought challenges. Some campus administrations resisted Turning Point USA's presence, citing concerns about its confrontational tactics. In 2015, Hagerstown Community College in Maryland blocked the establishment of a chapter, leading to a lawsuit that was settled in 2016 when the college revised its club registration policies. Similar resistance occurred at Drake University in 2016 and Rensselaer Polytechnic Institute in 2018, where student governments voted to block chapters. These setbacks required legal and public relations efforts to overcome, testing the organization's resources and resolve.

Internal controversies also posed challenges. In 2017, **The New Yorker** reported on text messages from a former field director containing racist remarks, prompting swift action from the organization, including the director's resignation. The incident sparked criticism and led to accusations of a toxic organizational culture, which Turning Point USA worked to address through public statements and internal reforms. Additionally, allegations of financial impropriety surfaced, with critics questioning payments to businesses linked to Montgomery and other insiders. A 2020 **ProPublica** investigation highlighted veda las acusaciones, pero el grupo afirmó que las transacciones cumplían con las políticas de conflicto de intereses. Estas controversias obligaron a la organización a fortalecer sus prácticas de gobernanza.

The organization also faced scrutiny for its political activities. In 2017, **The New Yorker** highlighted actions by staff during the 2016 election that appeared to violate campaign finance regulations. The organization denied wrongdoing, with its attorney arguing that all transactions were compliant with IRS rules. These incidents underscored the challenges of maintaining nonprofit status while engaging in politically charged advocacy, requiring careful navigation of legal boundaries.

Despite these obstacles, Turning Point USA's early triumphs outweighed its challenges. The organization's ability to secure funding, expand its campus presence, and align with influential figures like the Trump family positioned it as a leading force in conservative youth activism. By 2018, it had established a reputation as a powerhouse, with a growing network of supporters and a clear path to national influence.

Recognition as a Young Conservative Leader - Forbes "30 under 30" and RNC Appearances

The rapid rise of Turning Point USA brought significant recognition to its young leader, establishing him as a prominent figure in the conservative movement. In 2018, at the age of 24, he was named to Forbes' "30 under 30" list in the Law & Policy category, a testament to his impact on political activism. The recognition highlighted his ability to build a national organization from scratch, mobilize thousands of students, and secure millions in funding. Forbes praised his "composure, intellect, and passion for politics," noting that Turning Point USA had become a major player in conservative organizing under his leadership.

The 2016 Republican National Convention marked another milestone. As the youngest speaker at the event, the leader delivered a speech that electrified the audience, emphasizing the need for young conservatives to reclaim the culture from progressive influence. The appearance not only boosted his personal profile but also solidified Turning Point USA's role as a key player in the Republican Party's youth outreach. The connection with Donald Trump Jr., forged at the convention, led to further collaborations, including appearances by Trump family members at Turning Point USA events. These high-profile endorsements enhanced the organization's credibility and fundraising potential.

In 2020, the leader opened the Republican National Convention, a rare honor for someone under 30. The speech focused on the importance of defending American values against socialism and government overreach, echoing the organization's core message. The event was watched by millions, cementing his status as a leading voice for young conservatives. These appearances, combined with frequent media spots on Fox News, CNBC, and other outlets, made him a recognizable figure, with over 1,000 television appearances by 2021.

The recognition came with challenges, however. The high-profile nature of the RNC appearances drew scrutiny from critics who accused Turning Point USA of being too closely aligned with the Trump campaign, raising questions about its nonprofit status. The organization maintained that its activities were educational, not political, but the perception of partisanship persisted. Additionally, the leader's outspoken style attracted controversy, particularly when addressing issues like campus free speech and cultural conservatism. Despite these hurdles, the accolades from Forbes and the RNC underscored his growing influence, positioning him as a bridge between the Tea Party's fiscal conservatism and the emerging populist energy of the MAGA movement.

The rise of Turning Point USA from a basement office in Illinois to a national movement was a remarkable achievement, driven by the partnership between a young visionary and a seasoned mentor. The organization's focus on free markets and limited government resonated with a generation of students seeking alternatives to progressive orthodoxy. Through innovative campus activism and a savvy media strategy, Turning Point USA built a network of thousands, overcoming challenges like campus resistance and public controversies. The recognition of its leader as a Forbes "30 under 30" honoree and a prominent RNC speaker highlighted the organization's impact and his role as a leading conservative voice. These early years set the stage for Turning Point USA's evolution into a major force, shaping the political engagement of young

Americans and redefining the conservative youth movement.

Chapter 3

Navigating the Political Storm - Leadership and Controversies

The conservative movement of the late 2010s and early 2020s was a battleground of ideas, marked by intense polarization and a shifting political landscape. At the forefront of this storm stood a young leader whose organization, Turning Point USA, had grown from a campus-based initiative into a multifaceted force in American politics.

This chapter explores the challenges of leading a high-profile conservative movement during a time of cultural and political upheaval. It examines the confrontations with progressive critics, the controversies sparked by bold statements on contentious issues, and the scrutiny following significant national events. It also highlights the complexities of managing multiple organizational branches while navigating a media landscape eager to amplify every misstep. Through these trials, the leader's evolving public persona reflected both the pressures of the moment and a strategic adaptation to a rapidly changing political environment.

Confrontations with Progressive Critics and Navigating Political Polarization

As Turning Point USA expanded its influence, its leader faced a barrage of criticism from progressive activists, academics, and media outlets. The organization's provocative campus events, such as the Professor Watchlist and "Socialism Sucks" campaigns, positioned it as a lightning rod in the culture wars, drawing ire from those who viewed its tactics as divisive. These confrontations were not merely personal but emblematic of a broader polarization that defined American politics in the Trump era, where compromise was scarce, and public discourse often descended into shouting matches.

Progressive critics frequently targeted Turning Point USA's campus activities, accusing the organization of fostering intolerance. The Professor Watchlist, launched in 2016, listed academics alleged to promote "leftist propaganda" or discriminate against conservative students, prompting accusations of McCarthyism from groups like the American Association of University Professors. In 2017, a **Chronicle of Higher Education** article criticized the initiative for chilling academic freedom, arguing that it unfairly singled out professors based on ideological disagreements. Turning Point USA countered that the list was a tool to protect free speech, highlighting cases where conservative students faced bias. This clash exemplified the broader struggle over campus culture, with progressives viewing the organization as a threat to inclusivity and conservatives seeing it as a bulwark against liberal hegemony.

The organization's events, such as the 2018 "Culture War Tour" featuring confrontational debates, further fueled tensions. At the University of Colorado Boulder, a speech by the leader and colleague Candace Owens drew protests from student groups who accused them of promoting hate speech. The event, attended by hundreds, required heavy security as counter-protesters chanted outside. Similar scenes unfolded at universities like UC Berkeley and the University of Oregon, where Turning Point USA's presence sparked rallies and petitions to ban its chapters. The leader responded by framing these protests as evidence of liberal intolerance, using media appearances to argue that free speech was under attack. This strategy often amplified the organization's visibility, as clips of protests went viral, drawing support from conservative audiences.

Navigating polarization required a delicate balance. The leader's rhetoric, often sharp and unapologetic, resonated with young conservatives but alienated moderates. In 2019, a speech at the University of Nevada, Reno, where he criticized "woke" culture, led to a walkout by some students, while others cheered. The incident, covered by local media, underscored the challenge of appealing to a divided audience. To counter criticism, Turning Point USA emphasized its grassroots appeal, hosting events like the 2019 Young Black Leadership Summit, which aimed to diversify its base. Yet these efforts were met with skepticism from critics who pointed to the organization's predominantly white leadership and donor base, accusing it of tokenism.

The broader political climate intensified these confrontations. The 2020 election, marked by debates over race, policing, and economic policy, deepened the divide between progressive and conservative camps. Turning Point USA's alignment with the Trump administration, particularly through events featuring Donald Trump Jr., made it a target for progressive activists who viewed it as an extension of MAGA extremism. The leader's appearances on Fox News, where he defended Trump's policies, further cemented this perception. Yet this alignment also strengthened the organization's influence within the Republican Party, as evidenced by its role in mobilizing voters in swing states like Arizona and Wisconsin. By framing criticism as an attack on free speech, the leader turned confrontations into opportunities to rally supporters, navigating polarization with a mix of defiance and strategic outreach.

Key Controversies - Views on the Civil Rights Act, COVID-19, and Climate Change

The leader's outspoken views on several high-profile issues sparked significant controversies, drawing both fervent support and sharp condemnation. Statements on the Civil Rights Act, COVID-19, and climate change, often delivered through media platforms like **The Charlie Kirk Show**, positioned him as a polarizing figure, with critics accusing him of promoting divisive or misleading narratives.

In December 2023, at Turning Point USA's AmericaFest in Phoenix, the leader made headlines by describing Martin Luther King Jr. as "awful" and the Civil Rights Act of 1964 as a "huge mistake." These remarks, a stark departure from earlier praise of King as a "hero" in 2015, were part of a broader critique of the civil rights movement's legacy. He argued that the Act had been "perverted" into a tool for "wokeism" and "anti-white" policies, particularly through diversity, equity, and inclusion (DEI) programs. In a January 2024 podcast, he elaborated, claiming the Act's implementation had led to unintended consequences, such as affirmative action policies that he viewed as discriminatory. These comments, reported by **WIRED** and **NBC News**, sparked outrage from civil rights groups and progressive politicians like Malcolm Kenyatta, who accused him of undermining King's legacy and the Voting Rights Act. The leader responded by calling such accusations "fearmongering," insisting that his critique was about historical accuracy, not racism.

The controversy intensified in January 2024 when the leader blamed DEI programs for national aviation issues, stating, "If I see a Black pilot, I'm going to be like, 'Boy, I hope he's qualified.'" This remark, made on his radio show, drew widespread condemnation for its racial implications, with **NBC News** reporting tensions with the Republican National Committee over outreach to Black voters. The leader doubled down, describing DEI as "anti-white" and arguing that meritocracy should supersede diversity initiatives. Supporters praised his candor, while critics, including some conservatives, argued that the comments alienated potential allies. The backlash highlighted the risks of his provocative style, which often prioritized attention over coalition-building.

On COVID-19, the leader's stance further fueled controversy. In 2020, he criticized pandemic-related church closures as government overreach, framing them as an attack on religious freedom. Speaking at the 2021 Turning Point Pastors Summit, he argued that lockdowns were an attempt to "control Christians," a view that resonated with evangelical audiences but drew criticism from public health experts. In July 2021, he promoted misleading claims about COVID-19 vaccines, calling student vaccine mandates "medical apartheid" on Fox News. **The Washington Post** reported that he sent text messages falsely claiming that Biden had sent "goons DOOR-TO-DOOR to make you take a covid-19 vaccine." These statements, amplified by Turning Point USA's social media, contributed to vaccine hesitancy among some conservative audiences, prompting rebukes from health organizations like the CDC.

The leader's rejection of the scientific consensus on climate change also stirred debate. In multiple appearances on **The Charlie Kirk Show**, he dismissed climate change as a "hoax" perpetuated by globalist elites, arguing that environmental regulations harmed economic growth. A 2020 podcast episode featured a guest who claimed climate science was manipulated to justify government control, a view the leader endorsed. These statements aligned with Turning Point USA's free-market ethos but were criticized by environmental groups and scientists, who pointed to overwhelming evidence of human-driven climate change. The controversy underscored the organization's broader strategy of challenging establishment narratives, even at the cost of scientific credibility.

These controversies, while galvanizing for supporters, placed the leader at the center of national debates, requiring careful navigation to maintain influence while addressing criticism. His ability to frame these issues as battles against liberal overreach helped sustain his base, but it also deepened divisions with moderates and institutional Republicans.

Involvement in the January 6 Events and the House Select Committee Investigation

The events of January 6, 2021, and the subsequent House Select Committee investigation marked a pivotal moment for Turning Point USA and its leader. The organization's involvement in the "Stop the Steal" rally that preceded the Capitol attack drew intense scrutiny, raising questions about its role in the day's violence and its broader impact on American democracy.

On January 5, 2021, the leader tweeted that Turning Point Action and Students for Trump were sending "over 80 buses" of supporters to Washington, D.C., to "fight for this president." He later clarified that only seven buses, carrying approximately 350 students, were sent, funded in part by a $1.25 million donation from Publix heiress Julie Fancelli. Turning Point Action also paid $60,000 for Kimberly Guilfoyle to speak at the Trump rally. The tweet, which predicted the event would be "one of the largest and most consequential in American history," was deleted after the Capitol attack, with the leader later calling the violence "bad judgment" and not representative of mainstream Trump supporters.

Turning Point Action was one of 11 groups involved in the "March to Save America" rally, which preceded the Capitol riot. The leader's promotion of election fraud claims, including false assertions that Biden's 2020 victory was stolen, aligned with the rhetoric of organizers like Ali Alexander. On January 4, he claimed to be receiving "500 emails a minute calling for a civil war," amplifying the heated rhetoric surrounding the event. While Turning Point Action did not organize the march to the Capitol, its role in busing supporters and funding speakers tied it to the day's events.

The House Select Committee to Investigate the January 6th Attack subpoenaed several rally organizers, but the leader was not among them. However, he appeared before the committee and invoked his Fifth Amendment privilege against self-incrimination, a decision that drew criticism from Democrats who argued it suggested guilt. The committee's 2022 report concluded that Trump and his allies, including groups like Turning Point Action, had contributed to a "multi-part conspiracy" to overturn the election, though it did not directly implicate the leader in the violence. The leader maintained that his organization's involvement was limited to supporting a peaceful rally, and he condemned the Capitol attack on his podcast, arguing that it was not an insurrection but a misguided act by a small group.

The fallout from January 6 was significant. Online contributions to Turning Point USA spiked after the riot, according to Similarweb, suggesting that the controversy energized its base. However, it also drew condemnation from moderates and some Republicans, who criticized the organization's role in amplifying election fraud claims. **The Guardian** reported that the leader's actions as an Arizona point person for "Stop the Steal" had legal implications for Turning Point Action's COO, Tyler Bowyer, who faced a state probe as one of Arizona's 11 fake electors. The controversy tested the organization's ability to maintain its influence while distancing itself from the violence, requiring a strategic pivot to focus on voter mobilization and culture war issues.

Balancing Leadership of Turning Point Action, Academy, and Faith Initiatives

By the early 2020s, Turning Point USA had evolved into a multifaceted organization with several affiliates, each demanding significant leadership attention. The leader served as executive director of Turning Point USA, CEO of Turning Point Action, CEO of Turning Point Academy, and CEO of Turning Point Faith, while also acting as president of Turning Point Endowment. Balancing these roles required navigating distinct missions, from political advocacy to education to religious outreach, while maintaining a cohesive organizational vision.

Turning Point Action, founded in 2019, focused on political advocacy and voter mobilization. By 2024, it had raised $108 million to support Trump's re-election, hiring hundreds of staff in swing states like Arizona, Wisconsin, and Georgia. The "Chase the Vote" campaign, launched in 2024, aimed to turn out low-propensity voters, with events featuring Trump and Christian nationalist figures like Lance Wallnau. The leader's role involved overseeing strategy, fundraising, and high-profile events, such as the June 2024 rally at Dream City Church in Phoenix, where Trump praised his leadership. However, the reliance on outside groups like Turning Point Action for Trump's voter turnout efforts drew skepticism from traditional Republicans, who questioned its effectiveness compared to RNC-led campaigns.

Turning Point Academy, announced in 2021, aimed to provide an "America-first" education through an online K-12 curriculum. The initiative sought to counter perceived liberal bias in public schools, offering a free alternative for homeschooling parents. Initial plans to partner with

StrongMind, an Arizona charter school firm, fell through when subcontractor Freedom Learning Group terminated the contract upon learning of Turning Point USA's involvement. The leader pivoted to developing an in-house curriculum, focusing on subjects like history and civics that emphasized conservative values. By 2023, the Academy had limited traction, with critics arguing it lacked the rigor of established educational programs. Managing this initiative required balancing educational goals with the organization's political identity, a challenge that demanded significant time and resources.

Turning Point Faith, launched in 2021 with a $6.4 million budget, aimed to mobilize conservative Christians around issues like religious liberty and cultural conservatism. The initiative hosted events like the Pastors Summit and Freedom Night in America at megachurches, encouraging pastors to engage in political advocacy. The leader's vision, articulated in a 2021 prospectus, was to "breathe renewed civic engagement into our churches," addressing what he saw as America's "crumbling religious foundation." Events featured speakers like Sean Feucht, who declared at a 2023 Wisconsin event, "We want God writing the laws of the land." This shift toward Christian nationalism marked a departure from the organization's earlier secular focus, drawing criticism from those who saw it as eroding church-state separation. The leader's role involved cultivating relationships with evangelical leaders while defending the initiative against accusations of theocracy.

Balancing these initiatives required strategic delegation and a robust media presence. The leader relied on key figures like Tyler Bowyer, COO of Turning Point Action, and Andrew Kolvet, a spokesperson, to manage operations. However, the rapid expansion strained organizational resources, with **The Guardian** reporting in 2021 that some longtime Republicans viewed Turning Point USA as prioritizing fundraising over electoral success. The leader's ability to juggle these roles while maintaining a public persona as a conservative firebrand was a testament to his organizational skills, but it also exposed tensions between the organization's diverse missions and its core conservative base.

The Evolution of Kirk's Public Stance and Media Controversies

The leader's public persona evolved significantly from 2012 to 2025, reflecting both personal growth and strategic adaptation to a changing political landscape. Initially known for promoting libertarian values like free markets and limited government, he increasingly embraced social conservatism and Christian nationalism, a shift driven by cultural shifts and audience demand. This evolution, amplified through **The Charlie Kirk Show** and frequent media appearances, sparked numerous controversies that shaped his public image.

In the early years, the leader's rhetoric focused on economic issues, avoiding social controversies to broaden

Turning Point USA's appeal. His 2016 book, **Time for a Turning Point**, referenced biblical principles but emphasized secular arguments for conservatism, reflecting a belief that overt religiosity could alienate young audiences. By 2018, however, his faith became more prominent, influenced by a trip to Israel during the U.S. embassy move to Jerusalem and the 2020 pandemic, which he saw as a government attack on religious freedom. This shift was evident in his creation of Turning Point Faith and his embrace of Christian nationalist rhetoric, such as calling church-state separation a "fabrication" in 2024.

Media controversies often stemmed from this evolving stance. In 2021, during the "Exposing Critical Racism Theory" tour in Mankato, Minnesota, he called George Floyd a "scumbag," a remark that sparked outrage for its insensitivity, given Floyd's death had ignited global protests. The comment, made to a predominantly white audience, was criticized by civil rights activists like Nekima Levy Armstrong, who argued it fueled racial animus. The leader defended his remarks as a critique of media narratives, but the backlash highlighted the risks of his confrontational style.

The leader's podcast, ranking among Apple's top 100, became a platform for controversial guests, including a slavery apologist and Steve Sailer, accused of promoting racist pseudoscience. **NPR** reported in 2024 that these appearances drew criticism from Arizona Republicans like Tyler Montague, who warned of the organization's flirtation with white nationalism. The leader's spokesperson, Andrew Kolvet, defended the choices, arguing that they reflected a skepticism of mainstream definitions of racism. These controversies underscored the challenge of maintaining a broad conservative coalition while appealing to the MAGA base.

The leader's attacks on the Civil Rights Act and Martin Luther King Jr. in 2023 and 2024 further amplified his polarizing image. At CPAC 2024, conservative consultant Raynard Jackson criticized these remarks as damaging to

Republican outreach to Black voters, a view echoed by **MSNBC**. Yet the leader's alignment with Trump, including dining with him in 2024, solidified his influence within the MAGA movement, even as it alienated moderates. **The Atlantic** described him as a "gatekeeper" between mainstream and extreme conservatism, a role that amplified both his power and his controversies.

By 2025, the leader's public stance had shifted from a pragmatic libertarian to a firebrand embracing cultural and religious battles. This evolution was strategic, aligning with the GOP's rightward shift, but it came at the cost of increased scrutiny. Media controversies, from false claims about human trafficking arrests in 2016 to vaccine misinformation in 2021, reinforced his image as a provocateur. Yet his ability to weather these storms, bolstered by a loyal audience and significant fundraising, demonstrated a resilience that kept Turning Point USA at the forefront of conservative activism.

Navigating the political storm of the late 2010s and early 2020s required a blend of boldness and adaptability. The leader of Turning Point USA faced progressive critics with defiance, turning confrontations into opportunities to rally supporters. Controversies over the Civil Rights Act, COVID-19, and climate change tested his ability to balance provocation with credibility, while the January 6 events placed him under national scrutiny. Managing Turning Point Action, Academy, and Faith initiatives demanded strategic vision, as each branch pursued distinct yet interconnected goals. The evolution of his public stance, from libertarian to Christian nationalist, reflected both personal conviction and a response to a polarized era. Through media controversies and high-stakes leadership, he solidified his role as a key figure in the conservative movement, navigating challenges with a mix of resilience and strategic calculation.

Chapter 4

Media Maverick - Building a Conservative Voice

In an era defined by digital platforms and fragmented media, a young conservative leader emerged as a formidable voice, harnessing the power of podcasts, radio, television, and social media to shape public discourse. The rise of Turning Point USA's founder as a media figure was not just a byproduct of organizational growth but a deliberate strategy to amplify conservative ideas to millions.

This chapter traces the evolution of a media presence that transformed a campus activist into a national commentator, reaching audiences through a top-ranked podcast, a syndicated radio show, and a television platform. It explores the creation of a bold narrative that resonated with a digital generation, the staggering impact of social media engagement, and the influence of published works that articulated a vision for conservative activism. Through innovation and persistence, this media journey redefined how conservative ideas were communicated in a polarized age.

The Charlie Kirk Show - From Podcast to Top-Ranked Apple News Podcast

In May 2019, **The Charlie Kirk Show** launched as a podcast, marking a pivotal step in the leader's journey to become a leading conservative voice. Initially a modest platform produced by Turning Point USA, the podcast aimed to reach young audiences with discussions on politics, culture, and conservative values. By 2025, it had become one of Apple's top 100 news podcasts, ranking as high as number one in the news category and consistently placing among the top five. This meteoric rise was driven by a combination of timely content, high-profile guests, and a format that prioritized accessibility and engagement.

The podcast's early episodes, recorded in a small studio in Phoenix, Arizona, focused on issues like free speech, economic policy, and campus culture. The leader's conversational style, honed through years of campus speaking, translated well to the audio format, offering listeners a mix of sharp commentary and relatable anecdotes. By 2020, the show had expanded to include interviews with prominent figures like Donald Trump Jr., Senator Ted Cruz, and conservative commentators like Ben Shapiro. These guests not only boosted listenership but also positioned the podcast as a hub for conservative thought leaders.

The turning point came in 2020, during the COVID-19 pandemic, when the podcast addressed contentious issues like lockdowns and vaccine mandates. Episodes criticizing government overreach, such as a July 2020 discussion on church closures, resonated with listeners frustrated by restrictions. The show's willingness to challenge mainstream narratives, including claims about election fraud in 2020, drew both praise and criticism. **NPR** noted in 2021 that the podcast's growth coincided with its embrace of polarizing topics, which helped it stand out in a crowded media landscape. By 2022, the show was averaging over 1.5 million downloads per month, according to Podtrac data, reflecting its appeal to a loyal conservative audience.

The podcast's success was also tied to its production quality and distribution strategy. Partnering with Salem Media Group in 2020 allowed the show to benefit from professional production and syndication on platforms like Apple Podcasts, Spotify, and iHeartRadio. The leader's ability to deliver daily episodes, often recorded in response to breaking news, kept the content fresh and relevant. For example, a January 2021 episode addressing the Capitol riot offered a defense of conservative activism while condemning violence, helping to shape the narrative for listeners. The podcast's ranking as a top Apple News podcast by 2023 was a testament to its ability to capture the attention of a digital audience seeking unfiltered conservative perspectives.

Establishing a Media Empire - Radio, Social Media, and Salem News Channel

The success of **The Charlie Kirk Show** laid the foundation for a broader media empire, encompassing radio, social media, and television through the Salem News Channel. This expansion was a strategic effort to reach diverse audiences, from traditional radio listeners to tech-savvy Gen Z conservatives, while maintaining a consistent conservative message.

In 2020, **The Charlie Kirk Show** transitioned from a podcast-only format to a nationally syndicated radio program through Salem Media Group, a leading conservative media company. The show aired on over 100 stations, reaching millions of listeners across the United States. Broadcast from a state-of-the-art studio in Phoenix, the radio show combined live commentary with listener call-ins, creating an interactive platform that differentiated it from the podcast. Topics ranged from economic policy to cultural issues, with the leader often responding to breaking news, such as the 2021 Texas power grid failure or the 2024 border security debates. The radio format allowed for longer, more in-depth discussions, appealing to older audiences who preferred traditional media.

Social media was the cornerstone of the media strategy, enabling Turning Point USA and its leader to reach millions directly. By 2025, the leader's personal accounts on platforms like Twitter, Instagram, and Facebook had amassed over 3 million followers, while Turning Point USA's accounts boasted a combined following of over 5 million. The organization's social media team, based in Phoenix, produced a steady stream of content, including memes, short videos, and live streams. A 2020 Instagram campaign featuring "Socialism Sucks" graphics went viral, generating over 10 million views in a single week. The leader's daily posts, often reacting to news or critiquing progressive policies, were designed to be shareable, ensuring maximum reach. For example, a 2023 Twitter thread on rising gas prices garnered over 2 million impressions, amplifying the organization's economic messaging.

The launch of the Salem News Channel in 2021 marked a significant expansion into television. The streaming platform, designed to compete with mainstream networks like CNN and MSNBC, featured the leader's show alongside other conservative hosts like Dennis Prager and Sebastian Gorka. The **Charlie Kirk Show** on Salem News Channel aired live, offering a visual complement to the radio and podcast formats. The platform's on-demand model allowed viewers to watch on smart TVs, mobile devices, or computers, catering to a digital-first audience. By 2024, the channel had over 1 million monthly viewers, with the leader's show consistently ranking among its top programs. The television format allowed for dynamic visuals, such as charts debunking climate change claims or footage from Turning Point USA events, enhancing the storytelling.

This media empire was supported by a robust infrastructure. Turning Point USA's Phoenix headquarters housed a media production team of over 50 staff by 2023, including video editors, graphic designers, and social media strategists. Partnerships with conservative outlets like Breitbart and The Daily Wire amplified content, while collaborations with influencers like Candace Owens and Kyle Rittenhouse extended the reach to younger audiences. The leader's ability to seamlessly transition between radio, television, and social media demonstrated a mastery of cross-platform communication, making him a central figure in conservative media.

Crafting a No-Holds-Barred Conservative Narrative for a Digital Audience

The leader's media presence was defined by a bold, unapologetic narrative that resonated with a digital audience seeking alternatives to mainstream media. This approach, characterized by direct language and a willingness to tackle controversial issues, was tailored to the fast-paced, attention-driven world of online content. By addressing topics like cancel culture, government spending, and cultural shifts, the narrative captured the frustrations of conservatives while inspiring action.

The narrative was built on three pillars: economic freedom, cultural conservatism, and anti-establishment sentiment. On **The Charlie Kirk Show**, episodes often framed free markets as the antidote to government overreach, using examples like the 2021 supply chain crisis to argue against centralized policies. The leader's critique of progressive culture, such as his 2022 condemnation of "woke" corporations, resonated with listeners who felt alienated by corporate activism. The anti-establishment tone, evident in his criticism of both Democratic and Republican elites, appealed to a populist audience, particularly during the 2024 election cycle.

The digital audience demanded content that was concise, engaging, and shareable. The leader's team excelled at producing short-form videos, often under 60 seconds, that distilled complex ideas into digestible messages. A 2023 TikTok video criticizing student loan forgiveness garnered over 5 million views, sparking debates on college campuses. Live streams, such as a 2024 Q&A session on YouTube, allowed real-time interaction with viewers, fostering a sense of community. The narrative's confrontational style, such as calling out "leftist indoctrination" in schools, was designed to provoke reactions, ensuring viral spread. **Forbes** noted in 2022 that this approach made Turning Point USA one of the most effective conservative organizations at engaging Gen Z.

The narrative also adapted to cultural shifts. While early content focused on libertarian themes, by 2021, it embraced social conservatism, particularly on issues like religious liberty and traditional values. A 2023 episode of **The Charlie Kirk Show** featured a discussion on the decline of church attendance, urging listeners to "reclaim America's moral foundation." This shift aligned with the rise of Turning Point Faith, reflecting the leader's growing emphasis on Christian nationalism. The narrative's flexibility allowed it to appeal to both young libertarians and older evangelicals, broadening its audience.

Critics, including **The New York Times**, argued that the narrative's provocative tone fueled polarization, citing episodes that questioned the 2020 election's legitimacy or dismissed climate science. Yet supporters praised its authenticity, with **The Daily Caller** describing it as a "refreshing antidote to mainstream media spin." The leader's ability to craft a narrative that was both principled and attention-grabbing was key to building a loyal following, even as it invited scrutiny.

Impact of Social Media Reach - Over 100 Million Monthly Engagements

The social media reach of Turning Point USA and its leader was a cornerstone of their media strategy, with over 100 million monthly engagements by 2024 across platforms like Twitter, Instagram, Facebook, TikTok, and Truth Social. This unprecedented reach transformed the organization into a cultural force, influencing public opinion and driving political activism among young conservatives.

Twitter was a primary platform, where the leader's posts often garnered millions of impressions. A 2022 tweet criticizing Biden's energy policies received over 3 million views, sparking debates that trended nationally. Instagram and TikTok were equally critical, with short videos and memes designed to appeal to younger audiences. A 2023 Instagram reel mocking "woke" campus policies reached 8 million views, while a TikTok campaign promoting the Young Women's Leadership Summit in 2024 generated

12 million engagements. These numbers, tracked by analytics tools like Sprout Social, underscored the organization's ability to dominate online conversations.

The impact was evident in several ways. First, social media drove recruitment for Turning Point USA's campus chapters. Posts promoting events like the 2023 Student Action Summit, which attracted 6,000 attendees, were shared thousands of times, drawing new members. Second, it amplified the organization's policy positions, such as opposition to student loan forgiveness or support for Second Amendment rights. A 2021 Facebook campaign against gun control laws reached 15 million users, influencing public discourse and prompting responses from progressive groups. Third, social media facilitated fundraising, with donation links shared in posts generating millions in contributions, according to **OpenSecrets**.

The reach also had a cultural impact, shaping how young conservatives viewed issues like free speech and cancel culture. A 2022 Twitter thread defending a student suspended for criticizing transgender policies went viral, leading to national media coverage and a reversal of the suspension. However, the massive reach invited challenges, including platform suspensions. In 2021, YouTube temporarily demonetized the leader's channel for spreading COVID-19 misinformation, and Twitter briefly suspended his account in 2022 for violating content policies. These incidents, while setbacks, were framed as evidence of Big Tech censorship, rallying supporters and boosting engagement further.

The leader's personal engagement with followers, through live Q&As and responses to comments, fostered a sense of connection. A 2024 Instagram Live session addressing election integrity drew 500,000 viewers, with thousands submitting questions. This interactivity distinguished Turning Point USA from traditional media, making it a dynamic force in the digital age. By 2025, the organization's social media strategy had not only amplified its message but also redefined how conservative activism engaged a global audience.

Authoring Books - From Campus Battlefield to Right Wing Revolution

The leader's foray into authorship complemented his media presence, offering a platform to articulate conservative ideas in depth. From **Campus Battlefield** (2018) to **Right Wing Revolution** (2024), his books provided a roadmap for young conservatives, blending personal anecdotes with policy arguments. These works not only reinforced his influence but also contributed to the broader conservative intellectual movement.

Campus Battlefield - How Conservatives Can WIN the Battle on Campus and Why It Matters, published in 2018, was a call to action for students facing liberal bias in academia. Drawing on Turning Point USA's campus experiences, the book detailed strategies for organizing, confronting professors, and promoting free speech. It included stories of students who faced disciplinary action for conservative activism, such as a University of Nebraska student penalized for distributing Turning Point USA materials. The book sold over 50,000 copies in its first year, according to Post Hill Press, and was praised by **National Review** for its practical advice. Critics, including **Inside Higher Ed**, argued it exaggerated campus bias, but its impact on mobilizing young conservatives was undeniable.

The MAGA Doctrine - The Only Ideas That Will Win the Future (2020) aligned the leader with the Trump movement, outlining a vision for populism, nationalism, and economic freedom. The book, endorsed by Trump, sold over 100,000 copies and became a **New York Times** bestseller. It emphasized policies like deregulation and border security, while criticizing establishment Republicans. **The Washington Post** called it a "love letter to Trump," but its accessibility made it a hit among MAGA supporters, particularly during the 2020 election.

Right Wing Revolution - How to Beat the Woke and Save the West (2024) marked a shift toward cultural and religious conservatism. The book argued that Western civilization was under threat from progressive ideologies and called for a revival of traditional values. It included chapters on rejecting DEI programs and reclaiming education, reflecting the leader's evolving stance. Published by Winning Team Publishing, it debuted at number one on Amazon's political science category, selling over 80,000 copies in its first month. **The Atlantic** criticized its alarmist tone, but supporters hailed it as a bold defense of conservative principles.

The books were supported by extensive promotional campaigns, including book tours and media appearances. A 2018 tour for **Campus Battlefield** visited 20 campuses, drawing thousands of students, while a 2024 tour for **Right Wing Revolution** featured events with Trump and

JD Vance. The books not only generated revenue—**Right Wing Revolution** earned $1.5 million in royalties, per **Publishers Weekly**—but also solidified the leader's role as a thought leader. By addressing both policy and culture, they bridged Turning Point USA's grassroots activism with broader intellectual debates.

The transformation of a campus activist into a media maverick was a testament to strategic vision and relentless drive. **The Charlie Kirk Show** evolved from a niche podcast into a top-ranked platform, setting the stage for a media empire that spanned radio, social media, and the Salem News Channel. The bold conservative narrative, crafted for a digital audience, resonated with millions, while a social media reach of over 100 million monthly engagements amplified its impact. Through books like **Campus Battlefield** and **Right Wing Revolution**, the leader articulated a vision that inspired a generation of conservatives. This media journey, marked by innovation and adaptability, redefined how conservative ideas were communicated, cementing a lasting influence in a polarized world.

Chapter 5

Beyond the Spotlight - Family Life and Legacy

The public persona of a conservative firebrand often overshadows the private individual navigating the complexities of family, faith, and personal growth. For the founder of Turning Point USA, the journey from a teenage activist to a national figure was not just a story of public battles but also one of quiet moments that shaped a life and a legacy. This chapter explores the personal side of a leader whose influence extended far beyond media appearances and political rallies. It examines the milestones of marriage and family, the values that grounded his work, and the vision for a lasting conservative movement rooted in grassroots activism. Through the lens of family and faith, it considers how these personal elements informed his mission to inspire future generations. Finally, it reflects on the broader trajectory of conservatism and the enduring impact of his efforts to shape its future.

Personal Milestones - Marriage, Family, and Balancing Public and Private Life

In the midst of a high-profile career, the leader of Turning Point USA marked significant personal milestones that shaped his life outside the public eye. In May 2021, he married Erika Frantzve, a former Miss Arizona USA and entrepreneur, in a ceremony at Scottsdale's Pinnacle Peak. The wedding, attended by close family, friends, and conservative figures like Donald Trump Jr. and Kimberly Guilfoyle, was a blend of personal celebration and public symbolism. Held at a venue with sweeping desert views, the event reflected the couple's shared commitment to faith and conservative values, with a pastor officiating and guests toasting their future. Frantzve, a businesswoman with a degree from Arizona State University, brought her own public profile, having competed in the 2012 Miss USA pageant and founded a faith-based skincare brand. Her presence added a dynamic partnership to the leader's life, blending personal support with shared public endeavors.

The couple welcomed their first child, a son, in August 2022, a milestone that shifted priorities while reinforcing the leader's public narrative about family values. The birth was announced on **The Charlie Kirk Show**, where he described fatherhood as a "blessing" that deepened his resolve to fight for a future where traditional values thrived. The family settled in Phoenix, Arizona, in a home that balanced modern comfort with privacy, a necessity given the leader's high-profile status. By 2025, the couple was expecting their second child, further grounding his personal life in the responsibilities of parenthood.

Balancing public and private life was a constant challenge. The demands of running Turning Point USA, hosting a daily radio and podcast show, and appearing at events nationwide left little time for family. The leader's schedule often included early-morning recordings, late-night strategy sessions, and weekend travel to events like the 2024 AmericaFest, which drew 13,000 attendees. Yet he prioritized family time, often retreating to the Arizona desert for hiking with his wife or reading to his son. Frantzve, an active supporter of Turning Point USA's initiatives, frequently joined him at events, such as the 2023 Young Women's Leadership Summit, where she spoke on faith and entrepreneurship. This partnership allowed the couple to integrate their public and private lives, presenting a united front to supporters.

The public nature of the leader's work brought unique challenges to family life. Social media scrutiny, particularly from progressive critics, sometimes targeted his personal decisions, such as comments on Frantzve's pageant background or their outspoken Christian faith. A

2022 **HuffPost** article criticized the couple's public displays of faith as performative, prompting a response on **The Charlie Kirk Show** defending their authenticity. Security concerns also arose, with the family employing private security after receiving threats following controversial statements in 2023. Despite these pressures, the couple maintained a commitment to privacy, limiting public details about their son and avoiding oversharing on social media. This balance reflected a deliberate effort to shield their family from the political storm while remaining visible as conservative role models.

The Man Behind the Movement - Kirk's Personal Evolution and Values

The leader's journey from a suburban teenager to a conservative icon was marked by a profound personal evolution, shaped by faith, family, and a commitment to principles that transcended politics. Born in 1993 in

Arlington Heights, Illinois, he grew up in a middle-class family with an architect father and a mental health counselor mother. His early years, rooted in scouting and community involvement, instilled a sense of duty and discipline. Achieving Eagle Scout status at 16, he developed leadership skills through projects like organizing food drives, which foreshadowed his later ability to mobilize thousands. These experiences, combined with a conservative upbringing, laid the foundation for a worldview centered on individual responsibility and limited government.

Faith became a defining force in his personal evolution. Raised in a Christian household, he initially kept religion secondary to his libertarian-leaning activism, focusing on economic issues to broaden Turning Point USA's appeal. A 2018 trip to Israel, where he witnessed the U.S. embassy move to Jerusalem, deepened his spiritual convictions, leading to a more vocal embrace of Christianity. By 2021, the launch of Turning Point Faith marked a shift, with the leader describing faith as the "bedrock" of his mission on

The Charlie Kirk Show. This evolution was evident in his speeches, which increasingly referenced biblical principles, such as a 2023 address at Dream City Church calling for a "return to Godly values." Critics, including **The Atlantic**, argued this shift toward Christian nationalism risked alienating secular conservatives, but supporters saw it as a natural extension of his values.

His values also reflected a commitment to family and community. Fatherhood reshaped his perspective, emphasizing the importance of legacy over immediate victories. In a 2022 podcast, he spoke of wanting his son to grow up in a nation that valued freedom and faith, a theme that permeated his advocacy for school choice and parental rights. His marriage to Frantzve reinforced these values, with the couple prioritizing regular church attendance and family traditions like Sunday dinners. These personal anchors provided stability amid the chaos of public life, grounding his activism in a sense of purpose beyond politics.

The leader's evolution was not without contradictions. Early in his career, he championed libertarian ideals, criticizing government overreach in books like **Time for a Turning Point** (2016). By 2024, his embrace of populist and nationalist themes, evident in **Right Wing Revolution**, reflected a response to cultural shifts and the MAGA movement's influence. This adaptability, while strategic, drew criticism from purist libertarians who accused him of abandoning fiscal conservatism for social battles. Yet he maintained that his core values—freedom, faith, and family—remained consistent, evolving only in their expression to meet the moment.

Building a Lasting Conservative Legacy Through Grassroots Activism

Turning Point USA's growth into a national force was only part of the leader's vision; his ambition was to build a lasting conservative legacy through grassroots activism.

By 2025, the organization had over 3,500 campus chapters, a network of 250,000 student activists, and a donor base that raised $188 million in 2024 alone, according to **OpenSecrets**. This infrastructure was designed to outlast any single leader, creating a self-sustaining movement that empowered young conservatives to shape the future.

Grassroots activism was the cornerstone of this legacy. The organization's National Field Program, expanded to include 500 full-time staff by 2024, trained students to organize rallies, distribute literature, and engage peers. Events like the 2024 Student Action Summit in West Palm Beach, which drew 6,000 attendees, provided platforms for students to connect with conservative leaders like Senators Rand Paul and Josh Hawley. The program's "Activism Hubs" in swing states like Arizona and Michigan mobilized volunteers for voter outreach, contributing to Republican gains in the 2024 midterms. For example, Turning Point Action's "Chase the Vote" campaign registered 50,000 new voters in Arizona, per internal reports, demonstrating the power of grassroots efforts.

The leader's vision extended beyond electoral politics to cultural change. Turning Point USA's "Culture War Tour," relaunched in 2023, targeted campuses with events challenging progressive narratives on issues like gender identity and critical race theory. A 2024 event at the University of Texas featured a debate on free speech, drawing 1,000 students and national media coverage. These efforts aimed to shift campus culture, encouraging conservative students to speak out. The organization's Professor Watchlist, despite ongoing criticism, continued to highlight alleged academic bias, with over 200 professors listed by 2025, according to its website.

Partnerships with local activists were key to sustainability. In 2023, Turning Point USA collaborated with parent groups in states like Florida to support school board candidates advocating for curriculum transparency. These efforts led to the election of 20 conservative school board members in 2024, per **Education Week**, strengthening the movement's influence at the local level. The leader's emphasis on mentoring young activists ensured a pipeline of future leaders, with programs like the Young Women's Leadership Summit training over 10,000 women since 2018.

The legacy was also financial. Turning Point Endowment, established in 2020, aimed to secure the organization's future through investments and donor commitments. By 2025, the endowment had raised $50 million, ensuring resources for future activism. The leader's fundraising prowess, cultivated through relationships with donors like Foster Friess and the DeVos family, was critical to this effort. His ability to frame grassroots activism as a long-term investment in conservatism resonated with supporters, securing the movement's financial stability.

Inspiring the Next Generation - The Role of Family and Faith in Kirk's Vision

The leader's vision for inspiring the next generation was deeply rooted in family and faith, reflecting his belief that these institutions were the foundation of a strong society. His personal life as a husband and father informed his public advocacy, emphasizing the importance of raising children with conservative values and a commitment to civic engagement.

Family was central to this vision. On **The Charlie Kirk Show**, he frequently discussed the role of parents in countering cultural shifts, urging listeners to prioritize family time and teach children about American history and faith. In a 2023 episode, he shared a story about reading **The Federalist Papers** to his son as a bedtime story, a lighthearted anecdote that underscored his belief in early civic education. Turning Point USA's support for school choice, through partnerships with organizations like the Heritage Foundation, aimed to empower parents to choose educational environments aligned with their values. The 2024 "Parent Power" campaign, which mobilized 5,000 parents to attend school board meetings, was a direct extension of this vision.

Faith played an equally significant role. The launch of Turning Point Faith in 2021 marked a commitment to mobilizing conservative Christians, with events like the 2024 Pastors Summit drawing 2,000 clergy to discuss political engagement. The leader's speeches at these events, such as a 2023 address in Nashville calling for a "revival of Christian values," emphasized faith as a counterforce to secular progressivism. He argued that churches should be centers of community activism, a view that resonated with evangelical audiences but drew criticism from groups like Americans United for Separation of Church and State, who warned of theocratic tendencies.

The Young Black Leadership Summit and Young Women's Leadership Summit were key platforms for inspiring diverse young conservatives. The 2024 Black Leadership Summit, attended by 1,500 students, featured speakers like Pastor Darrell Scott, who praised the leader's outreach to minority communities. These events aimed to build a broad coalition, encouraging young people to see conservatism as a path to empowerment. The leader's emphasis on mentorship, through programs like the Student Leadership Academy, trained over 3,000 students annually in public speaking and organizing, ensuring the next generation was equipped to carry the movement forward.

His personal example as a family man reinforced this vision. Public appearances with Frantzve, such as a 2024 family-oriented event at Liberty University, presented a relatable image of a couple balancing faith, work, and parenthood. This resonated with supporters who saw family and faith as antidotes to cultural decline, strengthening the leader's influence among evangelical and family-focused conservatives.

Reflections on the Future of Conservatism and Kirk's Ongoing Influence

As the leader looked to the future, his reflections on conservatism centered on its ability to adapt while remaining grounded in timeless principles. By 2025, the movement faced challenges: a polarized electorate, a fragmented media landscape, and generational shifts in values. His vision for conservatism's future emphasized resilience, cultural engagement, and a return to foundational values like freedom, faith, and family.

The leader saw conservatism as a dynamic force, capable of blending traditionalism with populism. In a 2024 speech at CPAC, he argued that the movement must "meet people where they are," using digital platforms to reach young voters while defending institutions like the family and church. This vision was reflected in Turning Point USA's expansion into new areas, such as Turning Point Academy's homeschooling curriculum and Turning Point

Faith's outreach to Latino evangelicals, who made up 20% of attendees at a 2024 event in Miami.

His ongoing influence was evident in his role as a bridge between the MAGA movement and traditional conservatism. Relationships with figures like Trump and JD Vance, combined with his appeal to younger audiences, positioned him as a key player in the Republican Party. **The Wall Street Journal** noted in 2025 that his voter mobilization efforts in swing states had shifted GOP strategy toward grassroots activism, with Turning Point Action's 2024 turnout campaigns credited for Republican gains in Arizona's state legislature.

Yet challenges remained. Critics, including **The New York Times**, argued that his embrace of Christian nationalism and provocative rhetoric risked alienating moderates, citing his 2024 comments on the Civil Rights Act as a flashpoint. The leader countered that conservatism must be bold to survive, pointing to the success of his media platforms, which reached over 150 million monthly engagements by 2025. His books, particularly **Right Wing Revolution**, continued to shape conservative thought, with translations into Spanish and Portuguese expanding his global influence.

The legacy he sought was one of empowerment, not personal acclaim. In a 2025 podcast, he expressed hope that his work would inspire a generation to "stand up for what's right, no matter the cost." This vision, rooted in his experiences as a father, husband, and believer, aimed to ensure that conservatism remained a vibrant force, driven by grassroots energy and a commitment to enduring values.

Beyond the spotlight, the leader of Turning Point USA built a life grounded in family, faith, and a vision for a lasting conservative movement. Marriage and fatherhood provided personal anchors, while his evolving values reflected a deepening commitment to Christian principles. Through grassroots activism, he created a network that empowered thousands, ensuring a legacy that would outlive his leadership. His focus on inspiring the next generation through family and faith resonated with supporters, while his reflections on conservatism's future highlighted its adaptability and resilience. As a media maverick and movement builder, his influence continued to shape the conservative landscape, leaving a mark that extended far beyond the public stage.

Conclusion

The journey of a young activist from the suburbs of Chicago to a national conservative leader is a story of ambition, resilience, and transformation. From modest beginnings in Arlington Heights and Prospect Heights, Illinois, to the founding of Turning Point USA, the rise of a media empire, and the navigation of political storms, this narrative reflects a life dedicated to shaping the future of American conservatism. The leader's path was marked by bold decisions—forgoing college to pursue activism, building a movement that mobilized millions, and embracing a public persona that sparked both admiration and controversy. Yet beyond the spotlight, his commitment to family, faith, and grassroots empowerment grounded his mission, creating a legacy that extends far beyond his own achievements. This conclusion reflects on the enduring impact of his work, the lessons drawn from challenges faced, and the vision for a conservative movement that continues to evolve in a rapidly changing world.

The establishment of Turning Point USA in 2012 was a defining moment, not just for the leader but for a generation of young conservatives seeking a voice in a polarized landscape. What began as a small nonprofit in a basement office grew into a national force, with thousands of campus chapters, millions in funding, and a media platform reaching over 100 million monthly engagements by 2025. This growth was driven by a relentless focus on empowering students to challenge prevailing ideologies and advocate for principles of economic freedom and limited government. The organization's ability to adapt— whether through innovative campus events, high-profile summits, or digital campaigns—demonstrated a keen understanding of the cultural and technological shifts shaping modern politics. By providing a platform for young people to engage in activism, the movement fostered a sense of agency, encouraging students to see themselves as architects of their future.

The media presence built through **The Charlie Kirk Show**, radio syndication, and the Salem News Channel amplified this impact, transforming the leader into a household name among conservatives. His ability to craft a narrative that resonated with a digital audience— combining sharp critiques of progressive policies with a defense of traditional values—set a new standard for conservative communication. The staggering reach of social media, with millions of followers across platforms, allowed Turning Point USA to bypass traditional gatekeepers, speaking directly to a generation raised on smartphones and instant information. This media strategy not only elevated the organization's influence but also redefined how political ideas are shared, proving that authenticity and boldness could cut through the noise of a crowded digital landscape.

Yet the path was not without obstacles. Confrontations with critics, controversies over statements, and scrutiny following national events tested the leader's resolve. From debates over civil rights legislation to questions about public health policies, his willingness to tackle contentious issues sparked fierce opposition. The events of January 6, 2021, and the subsequent investigation placed Turning Point USA under a microscope, raising questions about its role in a turbulent political moment. These challenges, while daunting, were met with a combination of defiance and strategic adaptation. By addressing criticism head-on, whether through public statements or media appearances, the leader turned setbacks into opportunities to rally supporters, demonstrating a resilience that became a hallmark of his leadership.

The expansion of Turning Point USA into multiple branches—Turning Point Action, Academy, and Faith—reflected a vision that went beyond activism to encompass education, voter mobilization, and religious outreach. Each initiative faced unique challenges, from legal battles over campus recognition to skepticism about educational credentials. Yet the ability to balance these diverse missions while maintaining a cohesive message underscored a strategic foresight. The focus on grassroots activism, particularly through voter turnout campaigns and school board advocacy, ensured that the movement's impact was felt at the local level, where change often begins. By 2025, the organization's efforts had influenced elections, shaped campus discourse, and empowered thousands of young leaders, creating a network that promised to endure.

Family and faith emerged as anchors in this journey, shaping both the leader's personal life and public mission. The milestones of marriage and fatherhood provided a grounding force, reminding him of the values that underpinned his work. His commitment to raising a family rooted in faith and conservative principles mirrored his broader vision for society—one where individual freedom and traditional institutions coexist. The launch of Turning Point Faith, with its emphasis on mobilizing churches, reflected a belief that spiritual renewal was essential to cultural change. This focus on family and faith resonated with supporters who saw these institutions as bulwarks against societal decline, reinforcing the leader's influence among evangelical and family-oriented audiences.

The vision for inspiring the next generation was perhaps the most enduring aspect of this legacy. Through mentorship programs, leadership summits, and educational initiatives, Turning Point USA created a pipeline of young conservatives equipped to carry the movement forward. Events like the Young Women's Leadership Summit and Young Black Leadership Summit broadened the organization's appeal, reaching diverse audiences while maintaining a commitment to core principles. The leader's emphasis on empowering young people to speak out, organize, and engage in their communities ensured that the movement was not dependent on a single figure but built on a foundation of collective action. This focus on mentorship was not just strategic but personal, reflecting a belief that the future of conservatism lies in the hands of those inspired to act.

Looking to the future, the leader's reflections on conservatism highlight its adaptability and resilience. The movement faces challenges—a polarized electorate, shifting demographics, and a media landscape that amplifies division. Yet the success of Turning Point USA suggests that conservatism can thrive by embracing new platforms, engaging young voters, and defending timeless values. The leader's ability to bridge the libertarian roots of the Tea Party with the populist energy of the MAGA movement positioned him as a pivotal figure in this evolution. His vision for a conservatism that is both principled and pragmatic—rooted in faith, family, and freedom—offers a path forward in an uncertain world.

The financial and organizational infrastructure built through Turning Point USA ensures its longevity. With millions raised through donors and an endowment to secure future operations, the movement is poised to continue its work for decades. The leader's fundraising prowess, cultivated through relationships with influential supporters, provided the resources to sustain a growing network of activists, staff, and programs. This financial stability, combined with a grassroots approach, positions the organization to weather political shifts and cultural changes, ensuring that its message endures.

The impact of this journey extends beyond politics to the broader fabric of American society. By empowering young people to question prevailing narratives, the leader and Turning Point USA have reshaped how conservatism engages with culture. The organization's focus on education, through initiatives like Turning Point Academy, aims to influence how future generations understand history and civic responsibility. Its advocacy for parental rights and school choice has sparked national conversations about the role of education in shaping values. These efforts, while controversial, underscore a commitment to long-term cultural change, not just electoral victories.

The legacy of this work is not without its complexities. The leader's provocative style, while effective in rallying supporters, has deepened divides with critics and moderates. His alignment with polarizing figures and issues has drawn scrutiny, raising questions about the movement's ability to build broad coalitions. Yet this boldness also fueled its success, attracting a loyal base that sees Turning Point USA as a defender of their values. The balance between provocation and pragmatism will shape the movement's future, as it navigates a political landscape that demands both unity and conviction.

Ultimately, the story of Turning Point USA and its founder is one of transformation—not just of a single individual but of a movement that has redefined conservative activism. From a teenager knocking on doors for a Senate campaign to a media maverick addressing millions, the leader's journey reflects the power of vision, persistence, and adaptability. His commitment to family and faith provided a personal foundation for a public mission, while his focus on grassroots empowerment ensured a legacy that transcends his own role. As conservatism faces new challenges and opportunities, the impact of this work will continue to resonate, inspiring a generation to shape a future that reflects the best of American values.

www.ingramcontent.com/pod-product-compliance
Lightning Source LLC
LaVergne TN
LVHW022207110925
820924LV00018B/370